David,
    Happy Bday Bro.
                    Steve

David, it has been
a long time sence
our "tea & crumpets"
day. I am glad
to be sharing in
your birthday
May all of your
wishes come
true. Love,
Shaun

NEW YORK
TRENDS AND TRADITIONS

PHOTOGRAPHY BY   TEXT BY

ROBERTO SCHEZEN   CHESSY RAYNER

THE MONACELLI PRESS

First published in the United States of America in 1997 by
The Monacelli Press, Inc.
10 East 92nd Street, New York, New York 10128.

Library of Congress Cataloging-in-Publication Data
Schezen, Roberto.
New York : trends and traditions / photography by Roberto Schezen ;
text by Chessy Rayner.
p. cm.
ISBN 1-885254-74-1
1. Interior decoration—New York (State)—New York. 2. Celebrities—
Dwellings—New York (State)—New York. I. Rayner, Chessy. II. Title.
NK2004.S34   1997
797.2147'1—dc21   97-28070

Printed and bound in Italy

Typography by Abigail Sturges

Front cover: Bill Blass Apartment
Back cover: Lee Mindel Loft

Pages 1–5: Chanin Building, Sloan & Robertson, 1929

CONTENTS

9 INTRODUCTION • *Chessy Rayner*

11 INTRODUCTION • *Roberto Schezen*

16 DONALD JUDD, 101 SPRING STREET

28 REGINA AND ASHER B. EDELMAN HOUSE

40 FRED HUGHES BROWNSTONE

48 JANE HOLZER APARTMENT

62 PETER AND BROOKE HAYWARD DUCHIN APARTMENT

72 WILLIAM AND REGINE TRAULSEN DIAMOND APARTMENT

80 MARIAN McEVOY APARTMENT

90 JANE WENNER TOWNHOUSE

100 NIALL SMITH APARTMENT

110 BILL BLASS APARTMENT

120 CRISTINA AND MARCO GRASSI BROWNSTONE

130 RICHARD FEIGEN APARTMENT

142 ANNETTE AND OSCAR DE LA RENTA APARTMENT

154 APARTMENT FOR A BIBLIOPHILE

166 MRS. ANTENOR PATIÑO APARTMENT

178 CHRISTINE ZILKHA APARTMENT

188 RICHARD HAMPTON JENRETTE HOUSE

194 MICA AND AHMET ERTEGUN HOUSE

202 PETER AND JUDY PRICE APARTMENT

214 BARRY FRIEDMAN AND PATRICIA PASTOR APARTMENT

222 LEE MINDEL LOFT

230 JUDY HUDSON TOWNHOUSE

240 BARI MATTES AND MICHAEL O'BRIEN APARTMENT

252 DANA NICHOLSON LOFT

262 ZORAN LOFT

270 CHARLES COWLES LOFT

280 LOFT FOR AN ENTREPRENEUR

20

REGINA AND ASHER B. EDELMAN HOUSE

Asher B. Edelman and his wife, Regina, have gathered together a spectacular group of artworks in their house. The collection includes a wide range of twentieth-century artists such as Cy Twombly, Joan Miró, Jean Dubuffet, Frank Stella, Robert Rauschenberg, Jasper Johns, and John Chamberlain. The simplicity and spare look of the furniture is what makes the living space so remarkable. It is comfortable, but does not intrude on the art. The wraparound bookcases in the corner of the library are the same color as the leather covering the Jean-Michel Frank chairs and sofa. Above the mantle hangs a painting by Miró. Pale gray furniture floats on a beige floor off to one side of the room, facing two large canvases. Two black pieces of furniture stand out in front of the Twombly. The colorful Robert Morris is a great contrast to the quiet of the white-and-gray Twomblys. Beautifully lit, the space is unique in its clean, clearly defined architectural lines. Asher Edelman's eye is precise and the placement of the pictures is clearly in the hands of a master.

FRED HUGHES BROWNSTONE

*T*he uptown brownstone of Fred Hughes, founder and chairman emeritus of the Andy Warhol Foundation for the Visual Arts, is a treasure trove. With a connoisseur's eye, he has surrounded himself with a wide range of furniture, pictures, objects, and silver of all periods and from all over the world. A quintessential Warhol of Charles, Prince of Wales, hangs in the hall. In the green sitting room, there is an altogether different yet beguiling seventeenth-century portrait with a spectacular gilded frame over a nineteenth-century Russian settee. Illuminating the room is a German Empire chandelier of about 1820.

In the master bedroom a nineteenth-century Irish sideboard supports three imposing statues: a pair by Antonio Canova and a carved, polychromed Chinese statue of a man. At the other end of the artistic spectrum is an amusing set of porcelain Mickey Mouse figures made in Japan in 1930—the licensed Disney knockoffs—which can be found in the study. A Charles X mirror from the Palais Royal of about 1925 hangs over a Neapolitan sofa of about 1815. In each corner is a black chest of drawers with corncob handles, which were made in 1930 and are replicas of Victorian originals. The center table with carved horse legs was made in America around 1845. An oil-on-canvas banner that reads "Lodge of the Order of the Odd Fellows, Nyack, New York, 1875–1900" runs the length of the mantle. A collection of Chinese and Japanese dolls is housed in a lighted cabinet in the library. On one side of the cabinet is a painting of about 1870–80 depicting the military records of Captain Thomas P. Beech.

Downstairs in the dining room is a cabinet designed by Hughes to hold his silver collection, which includes American, English, French, Art Deco, and Mexican pieces. To one side is a rare New York sideboard and cellarette, possibly from the workshop of Duncan Phyfe. Over the sideboard hang two souvenir scarves with the abdication speech of Edward VIII, which a Swiss manufacturer copied for Hughes to give away as gifts. The bright green and vibrant blue paint that he has chosen is very unusual and this vivid color scheme is just one of the many innovative ideas that make the house so original.

47

JANE HOLZER APARTMENT

*J*ane Holzer, a collector and friend to many artists, created her own East Side loftlike apartment. By opening up the space, mixing wood and cement floors and stripping the doors down to their natural steel finish, she has built a modern airy apartment in a run-of-the-mill New York building. Holzer's style is not for the timid or shy. Large works by Keith Haring, Robert Longo, George Condo, Julian Schnabel, and her great friend Andy Warhol cover the walls. An antique Japanese kimono stand is used for Keith Haring's motorcycle jacket. An eclectic mixture of chairs is strategically placed throughout, from Early American chairs to Giacometti to red lacquer Chinese. Strolling though all of this is a Lalanne sheep on its way to the kitchen. Over an early American table hangs a Warhol portrait of Elizabeth Taylor, and four Warhol portraits of Holzer make up a corner in the entrance hall. A nineteenth-century leather screen serves as a backdrop for family pictures, which are placed on antique Chinese leather trunks.

In the bedroom a trim steel bed on a pale wood floor dominates the space. A professional-looking dressing table is watched over by an early Warhol, and over the television is a piece by Francesco Clemente. Holzer has taken us downtown in her concept of using the space—but how lucky not to have to face the traffic to get there.

PETER AND BROOKE HAYWARD DUCHIN APARTMENT

*B*rooke Hayward Duchin, the writer, and her husband Peter, the orchestra leader, live in a midtown loft. As you walk in you are greeted by a baby grand that is often being played by Peter for their guests. Behind the piano, hiding a service elevator door, is a large piece of canvas that has been painted to look like a giant, paisley-patterned scarf. The architect Walter Chatham, with 1100 Architect, has made the hall, living room, dining room, and open kitchen area flow into each other so that you feel you are always in the center of the space. The living room's huge mirrors, which Michael Trapp found in Chicago, are from a circus sideshow and are framed with old crown molding. Fortuny lanterns are reflected in them and provide light to a round center table filled with books. A large painting from 1920 by the Czech artist Ludvik Kuba of the violinist Jan Kubelik hangs at one end of the living room.

The dining room, which has bookcases on three walls, is covered by a Turkish kilim. A French baker's table sits directly opposite the open kitchen. Making the division between the dining area and kitchen is an old French zinc bar that also serves as a buffet. The kitchen is generous in size since the Duchins love to entertain and Brooke Hayward Duchin is a wonderful cook. The bedroom, which has a view of the Empire State Building, has a huge mirror to reflect the New York skyline. The bathroom has an oversized window and an overscaled English tub from C. P. Hart.

Throughout the loft there is a large collection of ceramics inspired by Bernard Palissy, a famed French artisan of the sixteenth century who carved snakes, lizards, and fish onto plates and platters; there was a revival of Palissy ware in the early part of the nineteenth century. The loft is imaginative and quirky, filled with finds that are personal, which, in turn, make it unique and so much fun.

WILLIAM AND REGINE TRAULSEN DIAMOND APARTMENT

Regine Traulsen Diamond, whose husband, William, is a city commissioner in the Guiliani administration, had the good fortune to find an apartment designed by Janssen, the famous French decorating firm of the 1940s and 1950s. The gilded moldings, mantelpieces, mirrored panels, and doors, even the faux marble in the entrance hall, are all intact. The structural shell of the apartment is what intrigued Regine Diamond and she has brought her taste for and love of French furniture into play. In the meticulously arranged living room are four eighteenth-century Regency chairs and an Aubusson rug from the same period. Between a pair of chairs from Fontainbleau is a Regency mirror, which hangs over a Boule commode. To one side of the blue banquette is a painting by Hubert Robert. Paneled doors designed by Janssen lead to the dining room. The Boule clock and the room's paneling are both eighteenth-century. A gray marble fountain stands to one side of the dining table.

Regine Diamond's Moroccan heritage shows through in the small inviting sitting room she has created. The banquettes are covered with pillows sewn by young girls for their trousseaus. The centerpiece cabinet is Spanish, possibly made for a princess during the time of the Moors. The lighting fixtures come from the ocean liner *Normandie*. A Moroccan rug and lantern finish the room. It is the perfect place to have coffee after one of the Diamonds' famous and delicious Moroccan dinners.

MARIAN McEVOY APARTMENT

Marian McEvoy, the editor in chief of *Elle Decor,* has a unique apartment that she has done herself. The first step—knocking down walls—was easy and it gave her two large rooms perfect for entertaining. The ingredients are all there—a sizable kitchen, a fabulous dining table, and the space to set up glasses and drinks in a large hallway, plus a lovely bedroom to collapse in at the end of the day. Lighting for dinner is supplied by a silver chandelier suspended over the table, which casts flattering candlelight on her guests. The book-lined alcove off the front hall, which can be used for smaller dinners or for drinks, is quite useful. The pièce de resistance is the extraordinary shell work that McEvoy has done herself around the ceiling, moldings, mantles, bookcases, and even the trunk at the foot of her bed. The painstaking hours it took her are unbelievable, but it was well worth it. There is not a spot untouched. The variety of shells and their patterns change from room to room. McEvoy orders the shells from India in large hundred-pound bags, and armed with a glue gun—there goes the afternoon!

With yellow walls, dark floors, white covered furniture, and black-and-white images on the walls the look of the apartment is dramatic and strong. Other highlights include the large, round, dining room table painted by McEvoy in a black-and-white primitive design and a rug by Christine van der Hurd at the other end of the room that sets off the black baby grand piano.

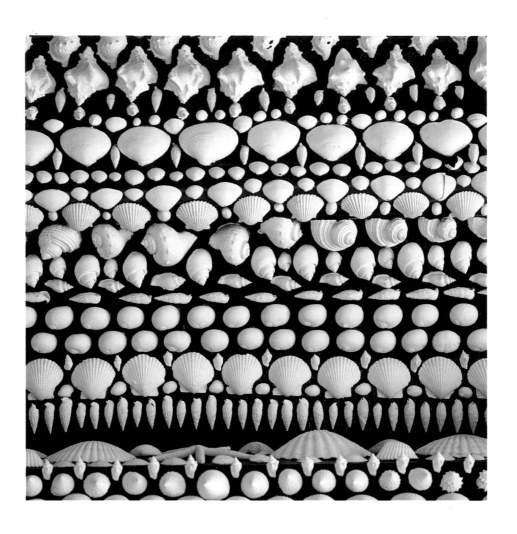

94

NIALL SMITH APARTMENT

Niall Smith, the Irish antiques dealer, has been in a midtown loft for the last eighteen years. He started his career dealing in Biedermeier pieces and later expanded into Continental furniture. The space he found was huge and wide open. He cut off the dining room space by placing an antique U-shaped bookcase at one end, which creates a library/dining room area that is one of the more appealing spaces in a house today. The entrance has a Biedermeier secretaire against one wall with a matching armoire across from it. To define the living room, Smith found at auction a Portuguese needlepoint rug that belonged to Nancy Lancaster, who had made it from the design of the front hall ceiling at Ditchley. It is a beauty and a perfect foil for the furniture. There is a Schinkel table with a collection of eighteenth- and nineteenth-century neoclassical urns. A collection of nineteenth-century Berlin ironwork sits on an Italian table with a scagliola top. Yet another tabletop is filled with a group of Grand Tour Sienna marble architectural elements.

Smith's superb eye for unique objects is equally discriminating with furniture. In the dining room, a Biedermeier armoire is flanked by a pair of Biedermeier vitrines topped off with Wedgwood urns. The metal chairs around the Biedermeier dining table are French Art Nouveau. The appeal of Smith's loft lies in his use of Biedermeier antiques with a mix of French and English pieces, which has created a light and airy feeling, the key element of loft living today. He has proved that modern minimalism is not the only way to go.

BILL BLASS APARTMENT

*F*ashion designer Bill Blass, a man with an eye for line and proportion, has employed his considerable talents to distinct advantage in his New York apartment. The entry hall was enlarged into an octagonal shape that serves as a gallery for his collection of architectural drawings. The cross-hatching of the wood and stone floor leads dramatically to the bare wood floors of the living room and bedroom. What is unique about Blass's space is that he converted the library directly off the living room into his bedroom. The door is open, so that when you enter you are drawn toward the bedroom. Fortunately, he is neat as a pin, so it works well. Blass's scheme makes for a superb room with bookshelves, a large, comfortable sofa, a working fireplace, and a large table that serves as a desk. The unsightly view from the window is obscured by shutters that are permanently closed. Drawings and watercolors are hung on them so that they simply act as another decorative wall.

Blass has used a unique mix of styles and periods to furnish his space. Swedish steel chairs are in the foyer, Italian consoles in the living room, and a round Irish center table is a stand-out piece in the bedroom. Antiquities abound, from Roman torsos to sixth-century B.C. Greek helmets. A Swedish desk with cloven hoofs adds considerable panache. It is eclectic, to say the least, but it all adds up to an unusual and brilliant mix.

CRISTINA AND MARCO GRASSI
BROWNSTONE

Marco Grassi, a fine arts conservator, and his wife, Cristina, live in a nineteenth-century New York brownstone. They have filled the house with mostly Italian furniture and paintings of the fifteenth, sixteenth, and seventeenth centuries. In the entrance hall there is an early-fifteenth-century Siennese gold ground painting hung over a sixteenth-century Tuscan credenza. Over the mantle in the living room is an architectural painting by Bigari with a pair of seventeenth-century still life paintings on either side. On the other side is a seventeenth-century painting by Castiglione and over the sofa is a painting by the seventeenth-century Florentine artist Dandini. These pictures are strong and they give the room a bold appearance. The imposing nineteenth-century desk is by the Englishman Henry Peters, who was a great success in Italy, where he was known as Enrico. The walls are covered in a printed fabric and the red carpet is a Savonnerie.

The dining room, whose walls are also covered in fabric, contains a pair of High Baroque carved and painted reliquaries. There is also a small console by Jacob with a gouache over it by Zuccarelli. Behind the dining room table is a view of Florence by Thomas Patch, an eighteenth-century English painter. The Grassis' related collection of paintings, ivories, bronzes, and furniture from specific periods is what makes their house so interesting, because they have furnished it with objects they love.

124

RICHARD FEIGEN APARTMENT

Richard Feigen, the gallery owner and avid art collector, has a charming apartment on Fifth Avenue that looks through the trees into Central Park. It is just like living in a tree house and looking down on the swings and slides of the children's park. Feigen's walls are filled with treasures that he has collected through the years. In the dining room, over the sideboard, hangs J. M. W. Turner's dazzling *Temple of Jupiter*. The chairs are Federal and were found in the Clarke House in Cooperstown, New York; the table, of about 1840, is also American. In a corner of the dining room is a group of Siennese paintings from the fourteenth, fifteenth, and early sixteenth centuries. In the downstairs library are a pair of chairs and a sofa by Le Corbusier. The pale green fabric walls are lined with a wonderful collection of Max Beckmann paintings and in one corner a Dubuffet keeps company with a painting by Rubens on a stand. Next to the library is the living room, where the walls are covered in a pale shrimp fabric. The carpet here is a silk Tabriz and the furniture is upholstered in a bottle-green velour. Over the mantle is another Turner, this one titled *Ancient Italy*. On either side of the mantle are four pieces by Richard Parkes Bonington. Upstairs there is a bright, coral-painted library that was hand-painted by Lucretia Moroni, who also designed the apartment. Over the mantle is a Baron Gerard; opposite it, between the bookcases, is a painting by Gentilesceu Danaë. The strong color of the walls makes the room very inviting and the books add to its charm. The cool background colors that Feigen has chosen to show off his pictures are a perfect complement to his justly famous collection.

ANNETTE AND OSCAR DE LA RENTA APARTMENT

*A*nnette and Oscar de la Renta have managed to take the library, dining room, and living room of a standard Park Avenue apartment and turned them into a Soho loft. By knocking down the two walls between the three rooms, their architect, Thierry Despont, created one spectacular space. One enters the library, which has a fireplace at the far end, moves into the living room, with yet another fireplace, and beyond lies the dining room. Bookcases mark the beginning and end of the three spaces, and since one can see over these bookcases it gives the effect of one large room. It is a brilliant idea and makes an old-fashioned layout work with today's concept that space is the ultimate luxury.

There is a wonderful mix of English, French, and Italian furniture and rugs, which gives this room a spirited personality and a look that is very much unto itself. In addition it is a space that looks distinctive day or evening. At night all the silver glistens in the candlelight. By day sunlight permeates the three spaces, giving natural illumination to a serene still life of white- and deep-purple-centered anemones in a lovely Celadon bowl. The two full-length, beautifully framed paintings of imposing Elizabethan ladies and two gentlemen facing one another at each end of the room anchor the space. And the entry into this wonderland? A long hall with a lavish mirror and a large painting of India by Edward Lear.

APARTMENT FOR A BIBLIOPHILE

An avid book collector has turned a double-height living room into a huge one-of-a-kind library. The books are displayed on shelving that covers every available inch of wall space from the floor to the fifteen-foot-high ceiling. Mark Hampton, who designed this spectacular room, and the rest of the apartment as well, says, "I have worked for twenty-five years with this client and the projects have always ranked among the most exciting of my career. The great Neoclassical library is, I suppose, the culmination of all our efforts over the years. In my opinion it possesses all the characteristics that make a great room. The furniture, objects, and pictures are all of terrific quality. Nothing uncomfortable exists in the room. And the owner's celebrated book collection forms a fabulous backdrop for the whole thing."

As large as this library is, it still has a warm, inviting atmosphere. Aside from the books, there is a multitude of objets d'art that Hampton's client has accumulated through time, which show a good deal of discrimination and a love of the hunt. No matter what the object, it is a delight to see the sharpness of this connoisseur's eye. On the tables one can examine rare ivories, antique bronzes, architectural stair models, and Egyptian heads. Breaking up the wall of books is a selection of original drawings that the collector has hung from the shelves. A warm red, patterned rug unites the whole room, creating a truly inviting and handsome space.

154

157

158

MRS. ANTENOR PATIÑO APARTMENT

Mrs. Antenor Patiño, an international collector, has a beautiful Fifth Avenue apartment with a decidedly European air, designed by François Catroux and the late Vincent Fourcade. The spacious entry hall with its black-and-white marble floor has red-velvet-covered walls and two large oils by Nicola Casissa. Leading into the paneled living room a de Hundecoeter painting hangs over a French bookcase. At one end of the space two eighteenth-century Swedish needlepoint screens stand guard by the library doors. In front of them are two covered tables with pictures by a follower of Carle van Loo. The far end of the living room is dominated by a pair of eighteenth-century bookcases on either side of Rembrandt's *Portrait of a Lady*. The dining room table is signed by Jacob and the silver dishes and cloches are Russian. Flanking the doors to the living room are two English consoles with a collection of antique French silver. The walls have old Chinese wallpaper that Mrs. Patiño bought from the previous owners.

The library is warm and inviting with red velvet walls that highlight a lovely French rolltop desk of about 1797. The romantic bedroom designed by Catroux has a charming bed with matching fabric-covered walls. Over the sofa is a picture of Mrs. Patiño's mother done by Lazlo. This is a lovely apartment that catches the afternoon sun, which makes it a cozy refuge.

CHRISTINE ZILKHA APARTMENT

*C*hristine Zilkha, collector of European antiques, lives in a charming duplex apartment on the East Side that gives one the feeling of living in a private house. This appealing European-inspired space was decorated by Jorge Latelier Yavan. A gray-and-white striped wallpaper with matching gray-and-white marble tiled floor in the front hall establishes the formal air of this apartment. Here you can find an eighteenth-century French barometer surrounded by pictures including a postcard by Saul Steinberg. In the living room a covered table in the center stands on a French turn-of-the-century rug. Stenciled wooden floors lead from the living room into the dining room, which has a view of the living room's fireplace, creating an enchanting effect.

Zilkha has collected furniture of different styles from many countries that goes well together. Italian consoles on either side of the Italian marble mantle in the living room, the pair of painted eighteenth-century Venetian armchairs, the dining room's Regency table with Louis XV chairs and Chippendale mirror all bring out the best in each other. In the upstairs hall an early Regency clock sits on a seventeenth-century Dutch Provincial chest of drawers. The theme continues in the bedroom with the headboard, which is made of eighteenth-century Italian gates with an Italian putto holding up the swag. On the floor is an exquisite nineteenth-century English needlepoint rug, and the night tables are a Regency painted country chest and a nineteenth-century poudreuse. It is a deliciously cozy apartment that is both formal and at the same time inviting.

RICHARD HAMPTON JENRETTE HOUSE

*O*ne of the prettiest houses in New York City belongs to Richard Hampton Jenrette, a longtime and well-known collector of American furniture and author of *The Contrarian Manager*. The front hall is a square space with nineteenth-century French wallpaper panels by Dufour and Leroy. A round center table from Boston of about 1815 and a fine classical carved giltwood sofa of about 1820 are the two main pieces of furniture in the room. Opening off the hall is an oval dining room with a beautifully patterned marble floor. In the four curved corners are niches with marble busts of William Pitt, the Duke of Wellington, and former British prime minister Spencer Percival. A lovely New York girandole mirror with four candelabra arms of about 1810 hangs over a New York sideboard attributed to Duncan Phyfe of about 1820. Also attributed to Phyfe are the dining chairs and the mahogany breakfast table. Over the mantle is an 1819 portrait of Daniel Tompkins painted by Charles Willson Peale while Tompkins was vice president under James Monroe.

The decor of the house is still evolving. Jenrette has collected and concentrated on furniture from the American Federal and Empire periods made in New York from 1810 to 1840. The design and grace of these pieces are superb. And although many of the pieces are of museum quality, they add a warm and inviting touch to the rather formal-looking rooms.

MICA AND AHMET ERTEGUN HOUSE

Mica, an interior designer, and Ahmet Ertegun, chairman of Atlantic Records, bought their house many years ago, gutted it, and began again. The first-floor dining room was extended back to its lawful limit and completely glassed in to the height of two stories. The result is a greenhouse-like room that allows light to pour into both the dining room and the second floor. Luncheon is always served at the garden end, and at night the entire room is used for dinner parties under the stars. Mica Ertegun (the author's partner in MAC II) has gathered pieces from all over the world to furnish the house. Mixed with the big dining room table from Russia and the German chairs are a painting by Adolph Gottlieb and a sculpture by David Smith.

Upstairs, the typical center hall with a room on either side was transformed into one large sitting room that overlooks the dining room below. Over the sofa hangs a Morgan Russell picture that was shown in Munich in 1912 on the occasion of the first American abstract art exhibition. On the walls a pair of gilt Georgian mirrors hangs over the fireplaces and is flanked by canvases by Ellsworth Kelly and David Hockney. Here, Biedermeier sofas are mixed with Jacobean pull-up chairs. The gilt table next to the sofa is Russian. The room is airy even when forty people are relaxing after dinner. Further up, in the library, a Bessabarian rug is surrounded by Russian Constructivist watercolors and drawings that liven up the fireplace wall. A Henry Moore bronze rests on the table behind the sofa. That all these seemingly disparate pieces go together may be due to the fact that Mica is Romanian and Ahmet was born in Turkey—a wonderful mixture of cultures that is reflected in their house, on which they have collaborated through the years.

PETER AND JUDY PRICE APARTMENT

*T*elevision executive Peter Price and his wife, magazine publisher Judy Price, have lived in this beautifully serene, Japanese-inspired space for close to eighteen years. It is a tribute to their architect-designer Cleo Nichols that there has been no need to change or update the look. Treading the narrow path of minimalism, good line, and quality he has achieved a lasting look that is comfortable and fills the Prices' needs. As you enter you are faced with a nineteenth-century Burmese votive statue backed by Shoji-screen-covered windows. The golden glow of a column and a marble pathway lead you into the next room. At the end of the living room two leather sofas face the fireplace; Ed Ruscha's 1969 *Standard Oil* stands on the hearth next to it. At the back of the room is an early-eighteenth-century Edo screen from Kyoto. In the corner stands a sandstone Ottoman monkey god from the ninth century. The dining area with its 1930 Jacques Emil Ruhlman dining table and chairs is at the other end of the room. On one side an Etruscan stone carving stands next to a painting by Cho duh Hyan. The front hall, a large and wide space, has a black and gilded gong designed by Jean Dunand in 1930.

The eclectic feeling continues throughout with a fourth century B.C. Etruscan watering vessel on a stand, a chieftain's staff from northern Angola, and a modern photograph of the pyramids. The Prices have placed their own stamp on the space using varied objects from different cultures and periods. What ties it all together is their eye and love of texture, tone, and shape, and above all their enormous interest in all things beautiful.

BARRY FRIEDMAN AND
PATRICIA PASTOR APARTMENT

*B*arry Friedman, a gallery owner, and his wife, Patricia Pastor, a private dealer in vintage couture clothing, live on the upper East Side with their two children in an apartment that has been added onto as tenants have moved out. The end result includes the large dining room, living room, and library. In a faithfully restored space that is full of light and luxuriously expansive, Barry Friedman's collection of furniture is shown to its best advantage. The entry hall is notable for the unique collection of men's ties, many from the 1940s and several of which are hand-painted. The dining room table, consoles, and chairs from 1928 are by L. Jallot, a Parisian cabinetmaker. Standing on the Art Deco rug is a lamp by Boris La Croix for Damon. Above a 1940s T. H. Robesjohn Gibbings chaise hang three recent Sally Mann photographs. The library has a pale Art Deco carpet and a lovely desk by Jacques Guinnet with a photogram by contemporary photographer Floris Neusüss hanging over it.

The square corner living room has a beautifully restored ceiling and is a treasure trove. It includes a carpet by André Arbus, a pair of chairs by Jean-Michel Frank, and a fireplace flanked by a pair of Arbus chairs and a side table. At the far end of the room is a 1930 glass screen, with its images hand-painted between two sheets of glass by Ernest Boiceau. The sofa is by Jean Charles Moreau and the torso beside the screen is by André Bizette-Lindet. The children have a great playroom that is a glassed-in orangerie with direct access to the kitchen. The Friedmans waited several years to add on to the main core of their apartment but from what is seen here, the wait was well worth it.

LEE MINDEL LOFT

*T*he architect Lee Mindel's lower Manhattan loft is a very special space that has been superbly thought out to take advantage of the views to the north, south, east, and west. As you walk off the elevator into a rounded open hall, you are met with an amusing chair by Gaudí and a pair of chairs by Frank Gehry. A spectacular staircase of floating, curved, steel treads winds its way to the top floor. From the hall you see the dining room to one side and the living room to the other. At one end of the dining room is the kitchen, which has sliding wooden doors that hide the work area.

The loft has been designed by Shelton, Mindel & Associates Architect with Reed Morrison, Architect. The fireplace with a window on either side was designed by Shelton, Mindel as were the two leather chairs that face a black-and-white wall construction by Charlotte Perriand. The Shelton, Mindel dining table is surrounded by Josef Hoffman chairs. Overhead hangs a crystal Venini chandelier that Syrie Maugham designed for Lord Mountbatten. At the other end of the dining area are two chairs and a coffee table by Hans Wegner. A surreal black-and-white screen by Piero Fornasetti, which depicts a winding staircase, very much like the one in the entry that leads to the second-floor solarium, stands in the corner. The openness of the space and the views of New York are dazzling, but the loft is not cavernous and has been planned with the idea that a family could live here in great comfort and a lot of splendor.

222

JUDY HUDSON TOWNHOUSE

*H*ere is an old townhouse creatively updated for a family of four: the painter Judy Hudson, her husband, and their two daughters. They bought this house and with the help of the architects Cicognani and Kalla transformed a nondescript, dull New York space into a freewheeling interior. Together they redefined the layout, tackled the lighting, landscaped the garden, resurfaced the floors, and painted the walls. The modern and sleek kitchen takes up over half of the ground floor and has new metal-framed doors that let in the maximum amount of light. The dining table was designed by the artist Julian Schnabel and has a tile top. Over the mantle is a Philip Guston painting with works by Steven Mueller on either side. Going up the staircase, there is a marvelous painted frieze that was discovered under the old wallpaper. As the plasterer was putting on his normal pink base coating to begin the process of repairing the walls, Hudson asked him to stop. The unfinished walls now have a pretty pink sponged effect with the restored frieze near the ceiling. The living room is large and comfortable, with oversized sofas and armchairs and saris strewn about to give an exotic "Ali Baba" effect. The master bedroom has a four-poster bed hung with dazzling fabrics and a patterned tiger-skin rug from Tibet. The two tubs in the bathroom are a luxurious reminder of the 1930s, when the house was first built. The furor the two tubs caused at the time is said to have cost the original owner a shot at political office! The bedrooms of the two daughters are truly imaginative. Ricky Clifton painted the ceiling and walls for one daughter as an interpretation of a Moroccan harem. The other daughter has a Chinese wedding bed in her room. With this most recent renovation, Hudson has managed to make the house the perfect contrast of comfort and whimsy.

234

BARI MATTES AND MICHAEL O'BRIEN APARTMENT

*A*fter much searching, Bari Mattes and Michael O'Brien, both lawyers, found their dream space in an apartment on lower Broadway with great light and an upstairs terrace for their dogs. The architect Dennis Wedlick designed the space to suit the owners' needs. It has a large living room, a small separate library/television room, a bedroom area with two baths, and an exercise space at one end. The apartment also includes a magnificent kitchen with plenty of room for kibitzers to oversee the chef and there is a breakfast area with a corner view at the other end. A specially designed staircase by Wedlick leads to the terrace. The owners like to entertain and can move Wedlick's tables and the Gijs Papaboine chairs to make any configuration that suits their particular needs. The carpets throughout were made to order by Christine Van der Hurd. The two chandeliers over the dining table are by Carlo Morietti. Between the windows are two pictures by Tom Slaughter. On the curved wall a television is hidden behind sliding doors and can be viewed either in the library or in the living room. The comfortable upholstered furniture makes the room very inviting for such a large space. In the library Wedlick designed cabinets to hold the owners' collection of Venetian glass, which includes pieces by Venini, Cenadese, and Carlo Moritto. The curved brown wooden walls add a certain dimension and style that give this loft a distinctive look of its own.

ZORAN LOFT

Zoran, the fashion designer known for his spare, beautifully cut clothes in luxurious fabrics, has used his signature style in a loft he designed for himself. The main attraction of this four-thousand-square-foot studio apartment with views in every direction is the light that pours in, illuminating the entire space. Zoran loves to wake up in the morning with the sun streaming in, so he rotates his bed according to the season—to the east in the winter and to the west in the summer. Floor-to-ceiling windows and a skylight let the Magritte sky be the never-ending ceiling. His shower, which is also airy and open, is illuminated naturally by a skylight, and the steel grid on the floor lets the water drain out.

Throughout the apartment a bright feeling continues with walls and floors that are covered with white epoxy for easy maintenance. A low, white table in one corner is surrounded by pillows on the floor for comfortable seating. On another side are steps with cashmere throw pillows. He does not even have a sofa because he wants his friends to feel they are somewhere other than New York. He has gone a long way in achieving his goal. His expansive studio is a wonderful and very special place to be.

LOFT FOR AN ENTREPRENEUR

*T*his downtown loft, planned for business meetings and occasional overnight stays, is very sophisticated in the use of space. Designed by Peter Marino, the square entrance hall is perfect for the large pictures hung on its walls. As you walk in there are two Schnabels on either side of a David Salle and a Francesco Clemente. Included in the space is a workout room with an evocative view of old water towers. In the bedroom hang a Jean-Michel Basquiat and, behind the bed, a William Morris rug; there is also an interesting array of Aesthetic Movement furniture dating from 1880 to 1900. Separating the hall and the living room is a large work area that features one of Warhol's Marilyn Monroe paintings over the fireplace mantle and is furnished with 1950s furniture from New York and Paris. Between the living room and the library is the game room, with Jeff Koons's basketball-in-a-water-tank piece facing a skylit pool table in the center of the room. Here the mix includes Richard Avedon photographs and furniture by Jean Prouvé and Charlotte Perriand with lighting by Royère. A spacious kitchen with many windows is used for business lunches and post-movie dinners. It is as much a sitting room as a totally functional cooking work space. Simple colorful dishes evoking the 1950s give the table a very festive look. The loft juxtaposes very successfully the art of today with furniture of the 1950s, showing each off to their very best advantage.